FLAME,
ASH,
FEATHER

First published in 2024
by Black Spring Press
An imprint of The Black Spring Press Group
Grantully Road, Maida Vale, London W9,
United Kingdom

Cover design by Matt Broughton
Typeset by Edwin Smet

BLACKSPRINGPRESSGROUP.COM

FLAME, ASH, FEATHER

A dozen eggs from Lockerbie

CATHERINE SWIRE

Winner of the annual
Best of the Bottom Drawer Prize

THE **BLACK SPRING**
PRESS GROUP

To Izaak Walton, my brother,

and the fearful who die in silence.

I wrote this short piece five years ago; neither the tone, nor the people, nor the chickens feel familiar now. However, I have decided to go ahead anyway – feeling it like a pencil suspended on a hinge in the wind. To those who it may upset, I apologise. I put it in for a bottom drawer prize and it opened – so I suppose the chickens needed to be let out. I am not sorry for the themes: the way men and women relate; the effects of sudden trauma on the mind; and, above all, the nurturing of fear that is part of power's promotion of terrorism. They have more energy than this small book can show; it is the obligation of art to work under them. Nor am I ashamed of the thought: particularly that of Arendt; and my old friend, Izaak Walton. My best hope, that the piece will encourage playful thought in others. To quote a dear student, whose work I am in the process of reading, 'We live in an era of misinformation... I believe if we continue to be excited by creation and the potential of authentic communication, there will always be good in the world.'

The terrorist event that resulted in my keeping chickens was the blowing up of my sister in a plane bombing. Thinking about that event now, I mean event in its fuller implication. That is, a massive collapse in the status quo that had propelled me through my childhood – a collapse brought about as much in one way by the victims as the perpetrators – and I use the terms advisedly, with Primo Levi's sense.

By my father who used the energy of the event to reconnect with his (estranged) family and simultaneously to launch himself into the media spotlight, conducting a straightforward, but resourceful and startling, search into who certainly killed, the one who had certainly died, for which the elite drilling of his childhood had prepared him. By my mother, who used the new storytelling opportunities to re-make her marriage, which was hitherto, as we sensed as children, full of suffering. Both my parents acted in response to the terrorists who put the bomb on the plane that took my sister out of life and also to the global media response to her death. Global media saw in it a satisfyingly absolute tragedy, a young, beautiful, white medical student, daughter of an affluent educated doctor and teacher, visiting her doctor boyfriend in New York at Christmas; a symbol of nuclear family, feeling fatherhood, faith, lone questers, justice, Englishness, Scottishness, and many other things.

So interested were they, that their vans filled our drives, journalists often filled our house, and the home we knew collapsed.

A collapse brought about most nearly, also, in my younger brother and in me; adolescents, still growing, and on the edge of adult life. In my brother, I cannot know, clearly, but I sense this collapse was cellular; according to doctors a tumour in his brain began to grow at that time.

In me, my identity collapsed, evaporated really, into the space and time of the moment, which was university, my first undergraduate year. When I think back to that time, I see it almost in Hiroshima or Nagasaki terms, personally, where the shadows of suddenly evaporated bodies were left burned into the stones. I almost became the people who were around me then; lovers, teachers, friends and as they slowly fell away into their own lives, the extent of my own internal detonation/absence became more apparent and destructive.

Falling on and on down through bonds I could not feel, I ended up, without any life that felt real or in any sense like my own. Withdrawn in a house bought with my sister's compensation money paid for by the defunct Libyan government (about blood money there remains a great deal to be said) into day to day relationships with chickens. I think of my friend Sara, beaten up by her father and ex-husband, who told me once, 'I think I like animals so much because I have given up on humans'.

Certainly, I found in these half reptile, un-mam-malian creatures, our closest relations to the dinosaur, a kind of kinship, a model, almost, of the relationships and patterns that were playing out in my head. A cadence of mourn-ing, of connective loss that makes me think of their company, over more than a decade, hold-ing and disappearing, almost mystically, like a smudge of feathered angels in the world, that held me to it, and observant of it.

It is only now, over a decade from when I start-ed owning chickens, having just handed over a cockerel the colour of flame and ash to a little boy, Nima, who arrived holding up the bird's printed out paper photograph from a website, that I see that the gaps between my life and my chickens' lives, the intense attention I gave to them through my youth, was perhaps not op-timum. That I have been standing outside and in, an emotional world, to which I was fright-ened to return wholly, because someone I loved, who grounded me, fundamentally with-in it, was gone.

And this early morning, in the silence left by the flame cockerel leaving, the connection, sound coincidence, in my mind between coop, the chicken pen, and coup, death's illegal seizure of power, comes to mind. Abject, I allowed the chicken's half alien forms to enter (safely) the torn emotional receptors of my mind. A coup in both senses, because it took up, illegally or improperly, as it were, the biggest part of my life, space, time. But also a coup in the sense of successfully achieving something difficult (with a little dislocation, certainly, a co-op, a mutually beneficial venture) a progression from leaving what I needed, my sister, to a life living with her loss.

In that context, I remember several times, over the years, friends who were achieving immense, worthwhile, practical things in the greater world saying, 'I just don't understand why you spend so much time with chickens!' My brother who, in the end, forced us back to visit the site of our devastation, in a different way, through illness, recently texted me, 'I don't get the chicken thing'. Right at the end of this time, a new friend, who I liked very much and whose strength in the face of her own loss I admired, told me she was very frightened of birds, that their feathers repulsed her. Her words signalled to me that my unthinking, instinctive attachment to chickens; my tracing their shape in poetry, which I have also done over the last decade, was something other than an admiration of angels. At the same time this friend took me to see Hokusai, whose ageing, persistent hands made and remade living chickens as art.

(Don't, as I begin on fears, get me started on my mother. She has, and I shared them very young, three big fears – phobias – a fear of trapped birds, of dead creatures and of lightning. Can it be a coincidence that all of them have defined my life? And under them, my own primary, imaginary terrors as a child, of the spirit world, which I believed, at six, used to visit me – and of dying without my family. I have one more phobia, a sensual one; the sound of hands running over synthetic woven cloth, but that may, or may not, count here...) My mother, who as the pandemic began, brought round a Tupperware box full of nineteenth century Japanese woodblock prints from my grandmother's damp Scottish library, including many of cockerels, many of them Hokusai.

So to stick firmly with the theme, I began to make a connection between my chickens, the spirit world of my childhood terror, and my own fear. There it is, of course, in the language, 'Don't be a chicken', 'I'm chicken'.

My fascination with chickens has been my game with death. Both with it and against it. Also my comedy. A way of coping with the central functions of life, while missing a vital component. I am going to try, with as much detail and precision as possible in a notebook, to show how. Please do not read this small book all at once, but take your time. Treat each chapter as an egg. More than three at one sitting is excessive...

1. I AND YOU

Although I lost pets in my childhood and mourned for them, sometimes for months afterwards, the death of my sister at twenty-one, so suddenly and improbably – didn't I, after all, share her bed the night before and travel with her to the airport, see her onto the plane? Didn't my clothes smell of her? Brought about the impossible reality of death, in all its unravellings, very, very close. I needed to learn more about it.

Chickens, half-flighted, food-farmed birds, are prey to so many ends, they have, or seem to have, a facility for death, more than many creatures. Before I kept chickens for the first time I went on a day long Poultry Keeping Course at agricultural college. We were taught many useful things. How to clip wings, for example.

You tease two or three main feathers out of one wing and snip them so the wings are unbalanced. Feathers are insentient, so the chicken is not hurt by its unbalancing, but it cannot fly far or high.

The college also gave us a printed list of Chickens, Ailments and Remedies.

Chickens have an impressive and poetic range of maladies, including Mushy Chick, Gumboro and Bumblefoot. The solution to almost all of them, according to the list, still in my drawer, is 'cull'. It is interesting how that sound slippage from kill to cull, from I to you, sanitises the act of departure. The delusion of self primacy that lies at the heart of fear (since at a level the loss of you and the loss of me, is really, more or less, the same). As in this title, the idiomatic order, you and I, is flipped by the dislocation of trauma, and the deluded primacy of the self, self absorption, tips us into the world of fear, into an acceptable difference between killing and culling. At the time I knew nothing about chickens, the complete readiness of instructors to abandon, rather than care for, their lives shocked me. I wrote a poem at the time, which is half-lost now. Reading it back, I can see it is full of quiet laughter. Here is what's left.

REARING HOME CHICKENS

It is their facility for death
that is remarkable; in case of
Vert Gleet, Perosis,
Aspergillosis, Gumboro
Marek's and Bumblefoot
just the one advice;
consider euthanasia.

Also for sleep. Apparently, you put
the head under the wing and
rock, two or three times,
and they go off; just like a light.
(If you introduce an alien to them in
this state, so long as there's good food,
why, normally, they let it live.)

As for the deed; various humane methods
a cone with chains; something much like a
hole punch; the axe, of course; experts favour
the pull and twist, which runs the risk
of the entire head breaking off; the throat's
so slight.

Truth is, the total value of one bird
equates to three minutes of
an expert's time (less if you want
drugs). Death then solves all;
but Scaly Legs (requiring surgical spirit)
or Angel Wings (which you can tape yourself).

And yet, I note; though, clearly our fowl merit
so few *living* solutions; their reptile origins,
among the dinosaurs...' ★

The poem goes on – somewhere – nowhere –
to dismiss Victorian hybrids and to focus on
the pleasant fantasy of rescuing those raised
by machines under light bulbs; giving them

freedom and a chance to lay – and I think, if I *remember rightly*, it was ten years ago – to question that. That part is lost.

Reading the poem back, I like the poem's beginning very much. I hear irony spinning in almost every word, an exhaustion with what felt like the almost voyeuristic fascination of what had happened to me in those around me within the academic community where I was studying, and a yearning to connect with animality. I also hear the voice and mind of my beloved teacher at Oxford for whom I think I wrote this poem; her despair, as I saw it then, at the fearfulness, and desire to encourage resilience and resourcefulness in her string of pupils, who revealed themselves, attached and then vanished, as rapidly and as helplessly as chickens. But under it, I hear the reasons that respond to my friend's question about why on earth I spend so much time with chickens and my brother's 'I don't get the chicken thing'.

Chickens, in a sense like pupils, simplify and reduce human behaviour because they place us in a position of control and power. Above all, for me anyhow, plunged into a situation of radical loss, which had very few comparable or obvious connections with those at university, young, beloved and lucky, around me, they allowed me very quietly to observe death – and mourning. Therefore, as quietly, to build a better understanding of whatever it was that had leapt on me suddenly, that had robbed me but that was also important – because it appeared to be what was left of my sister.

2. EVENT AND GROUND

One of the hardest emotional aspects of sudden death, particularly in a terrorist incident, or in any event which is completely unforeseen and off-stage, is that it breaks all sense of emotional flow and continuity.

For me the literal loss of someone I was physically, emotionally, discursively, close to and had grown with was re-inscribed by a loss of sense of any value whatsoever in my own feelings and intuition; the point where feeling touches brain – sentience. I suspect that my sentience had, hitherto, been fairly vivid because I grew up with a passionate, articulate, physically present mother and sister in the quasi countryside, with many animals. In one sense I was well placed, young and intact, I thought, to cope with the sudden deprivation;

better I thought, perhaps, than my parents, whose searching self narrations, were gobbled up and broadcast out by the sentient-starved, sentiment-hungry media. Safer, as it may have been, than my younger brother, at boarding school and exposed to his family (his home!) story remade as *sensation* (a word which invariably signals numbness, its absence) every night – without a sister. I was grateful as well as horrified by those who at Oxford, jumped on me, to rescue me, as they no doubt thought, with their strong spirits from an impossible public situation, where grief was compounded and inhibited by the complete fictionalisation of my home life. As well as observant of those who treated me as if I were contaminated. As if anyone can rescue anyone else from death!

We forgot in the scrum the oldest joke, why did the chicken cross the road?

I was game to learn. Quickly, ecstatically, I learned about 'the waning of affect', an adult world of emotionless will. An exciting flight of pure aesthetic dream, where for me anything was possible, since none of the sinews that bound me to the slow seep of the world, were left intact. As a result, at that time, I could connect with pure, radical thought like lightning and quietly accepted the accolades that accompanied that ability. But, I see this, quietly and ruefully, more than a quarter of a century on, in this bright break I was separated from all continuity, and left emotionally completely prone. In that sense, I was like a chicken, a herbivore, not a predator; frightened to show that I was weak. The high, white, perfect paradise of the mind is as much a graveyard as the thoughtless slurp of the body.

I leapt, without reflection, towards those drawn to me by narratives of disaster, who wanted, or appeared to want, usually out of their own abused or complex emergence, to save, or were attracted to the energy and glamour of external media attention. What else does anyone have after an event?

I remember one of my housemates, buying me carnations as my father appeared as the lead on the nine o'clock news, with another image, the thousandth, of my sister's death in a crumpled plane, at the garage trestle table draped with our sheets, our washing. She looked me straight in the eye, saying simply, 'It's exciting.'

The next few decades that should perhaps have been (I remembered this from the whole visions of my childhood) the time of growth and establishment, of display, romance and job, rather felt like a continued wordless falling away. From those who had hoisted high in a white space to save me from the public mess of my home, but who really had no more durable, reciprocal emotional attachment to me (as became clear, this is not the character of salvation) and, in the most extreme cases, no sentient attachment at all. No more than if they were books. Which, in a sense, in the absence of my ability to read, they were.

I still wonder now, if in fact they did save me, these heroes, lovers and gurus dragging me into their world of pure mind. Since, it would seem, though I am old, I have survived. But I observe that the cost to pay has been very high in terms of my own life. The default position of the one who has been rescued, is exile. Self silence, shadow, conformity. And fear. So, as we have seen, I chose rather to spend a great deal of time afterwards, perhaps skulking from my spirit saviours with their strident, self absorbed Is and their disposable Us, hanging out with voiceless feathered bundles, chickens like me, stuck, like me, in the pen. Watching how other living creatures managed death and trying to reconnect, I suppose, with something that felt taken, that had vanished. That I needed, in order to move.

Please note, I still have not killed or culled a chicken although I have just, as I mentioned, given away one, the colour of ash and flame, for free... (Since I was a child, I have felt instinctively against the dispatching of any life. I am, viscerally, passionately opposed, for example, to capital punishment in all circumstances. So deeply in fact, it is as if I myself were once the victim of it...).

I have however, now, lived alongside chickens dying for so long that I have got to the point where I can mostly sense, just by standing at the coop, whether a chicken has died. I do not know if this is because there is a kind of stillness, a loss of energy in the air around the coop, or because of the changed physicality of the other birds, or because the corpse itself, in its sudden, abrupt, unthinkable change emits some emanation or some absence.

Certainly I would observe that chickens themselves – and this makes the horror of how we treat them in industrial farming worse – given space – certainly mourn. A chicken I was hopelessly fond of (I try not to attach this way to chickens now) right back at the beginning, whom we called Pippi Longstocking because of her long yellow legs (and after the half socked orphan icon of my daughter's infant imagination) saw her white sister/companion eaten by a fox in the yard. She stood for hours afterwards, calling, calling, calling... Emptily, to nothing, since she had certainly seen what had happened. Shortly afterwards she appeared to do what, in a sense, we all, in my family, did after my sister's death. She moved out. Up high. Away. To the treetops. She would come down into the yard and join the other hens in the day, but at night she would not be locked up, she went early up into the woods on her own to roost, in a tree.

It felt like the brightest miracle every morning, when you stood on the step calling her and she came high-chortling down the wood path. Later we found tens of pale green eggs she had secretly laid in the hollow of a tree, they made me think of the, literally, hundreds of poems and essays, I have written, and hidden. Until, in the end, after months, the woods got her. As woods, in the end, will.

I still don't know if Pippi was, exactly, mourning her dead companion, or if her vanishing was rather to do with witnessing a sudden attack and no longer perceiving the yard as safe, blurring, as we all do the *event* with the *ground*. Another delusion of fear. Or perhaps if this blurring of fear is always part of the work of mourning.

Anyhow back to my own gradual intuition that a chicken has died, whether because of the other Pippi-like chicken figures, or because of something more metaphysical or environmental.

Looking back, I can see that I have been conducting the quietest of emotional experiments on what had happened to my sister and to me. Part of a work of mourning I was unable, because of the suddenness of the vanishing and my par-

ents' very public performance, which I now understand as a kind of resistance to mourning,
to carrying it out in other ways. A school friend
I'm fond of, I remember once wrote to me and
told me my situation was like that of Antigone.
Though I denied it, along with many things he
said that were fairly accurate, for its classical
heaviness, it can sometimes feel, that I have
spent these years, scraping holy earth, with the
chickens, over the body of my sister, re-learn-
ing death as process. Amongst the many, many
abandoned eggs, this half poem-note, weak in
itself, and full of puns and implications...

I honestly thought I could always tell
if one was dead by the feel in the pen.
A shock then, this one. Lifting the lid.
Big Ginger, unintelligible… flat as her feathers.
Her sisters must have stepped over her body to enter
the day run… hard to think about living hens
shut up behind the dead body of their sister.
Grey, quiet sprawl, liquid flat. I almost called
to some parent – 'You do it!'

After a while contemplating her flatness, her
absolute quiet, I got the spade, and,
with a shudder, many awkward turns,
twisted her towards the door.
Her scaly head lolled,
she felt closer to life
lifted in the air, a little stiff. I laid her then
softly in the compost, the evening
felt softer too, then, and separated –

3. ON FORGETTING

As a child, like many children, my voice evolved in passionate connection with my mother. She who was terrified of trapped birds, dead creatures and thunder storms. She seemed to me, as a child, most brave spirited, intelligent and cheerful with a strong spiritual sense or curiosity (which I guess evolved from not having a mother to guide her). My language followed her (lovely to me) body as it bustled round home and a part-time teaching job in a cheerful, perceptive, spiritually inclined sort of way. My religious inclination and my mother's regular practice of prayer with me in bed each night, primed me, I suppose, to express what there was no room for in poetry; language made alone but directed toward another. As children we owned a small dapple grey donkey, ex-brood mare at the local donkey farm, Tina (without a cross) and I would also lie on her back and talk/sing to her, in the manner of a prayer or song.

One of the shocking things about the sudden death of my sister and the fear it provoked was that my profound sense of bond with my mother broke. Completely. My mind involuntarily separated itself from her. In the fear that gripped us all, I suppose, in the days afterwards, a black line seemed to rise from the horizon and I felt utterly suddenly apart from her, analysing her words for their irrationalities, with the cool, cerebral tools my father's mind facilitated, as if I had taken leave of the ground and was circling above it. In a trapped, perpetual adolescence.

This aspect of grief, this black-lined separation from the earth, is I think what brought me so many problems in language and expression, both in my work at the time – a literature degree (I could not read!) – and in my friendships with the relaxed, language-fed, ambitious students at my university.

It also perhaps raised for me the very deep problem of finding language properly to interpret and hold difficult adult experience of trauma. If the language you have evolved until you are plunged in media res, in horror, has been uniquely responsive, as mine deeply, largely felt, to a loving and child focused mother. And if the sister with whom you were experimenting with far more radical and provocative thoughts, vanishes... Suddenly in my heart and attachment, alone, I faced sudden death and, really, active sexuality together. I see now that both my brother and I were dangerously lacking in a basic understanding of the language of adult emotion, especially mourning and grieving – and this led to many problems for us.

Oxford at that time, and ideally now, was a fundamentally positivistic and political culture; in the liberal arts it/we were concerned with revealing. Lighting shadows, upturning, remembering culturally, as well as personally, bearing witness.

It was not, perhaps, and I write this lightly, the best environment for burial.

Years later on, when I was no longer able really to study, I read Toni Morrison's writing. I was on a scholarship in Canada, trying to process words, but hardly opened an appropriate book, spent part of it in hospital because my blood itself clotted up ('blood too thick!') and managed, somewhat spectacularly, to get a z grade. Through it, I realised it was possible to make a shape, at some level, for what should not be passed on, for the toxic apolitical internal luminescences of trauma and unacknowledged grief and the way they disable us. How, even in this smile-or-die culture in which we live, such spectral negativity can still, with skill be represented or understood. I loved the novel, *Beloved*, because it seemed to me to make shape for that negativity. To allow in the deepest, most human shape, of blackness.

Decades after, I read Nicole Loraux, who took over Derrida's role at the Ecole Normale in Paris. Her studies of ancient Athens and, in particular, women's civic role (which was to mourn) seemed to develop Morrison's work in my mind and taught me, more vocally, how to imagine or make a space in my head away from what had happened; the language of forgetting. Loraux argues that the 'un-forgetful shall be the forgotten' and shows how forgetting was practiced in ancient Athens – to the extent that a day of trauma and disaster for the city was literally scribbled or cut out of the calendar; made into a white space or blank. Reference to the date was renounced by voting males, under oath, those who reneged, faced the death sentence. What processing there was then, of disaster, remained in the hands of the otherwise civically mute, the mourners; the women.

I drank Loraux's work about forgetting, about burial, like milk, under the media onslaught that continued for decades over Lockerbie –

even today as I write this, the story has emerged again, a new headline, a new suspect, the number of American deaths repeated – and the impossibility of mourning, of scraping earth over someone I loved and has gone is renewed. New acquaintances tweet sympathy and I, in my heart, remember everything that has happened and hasn't. Loraux taught me to think about the white blank, the white-out of forgetting actively – the work I needed to do, in order to survive, symbolically, as it were, gain access to a civic, vocal space, in an impossible situation, where I was not just defined by my sister, but by her death.

And chickens in their restless, feathery fear come in again. Not only did they symbolise that air borne flight of the mind, a white, cerebral flight (also a flight focused on goodness, white, blanche, symbol for purity – brain fluid's white, as opposed to circulatory blood which is red) from the sudden, violent death of my sister. But also the white ones, either White

Stars, or a certain type of hybrid rescue hen, often maimed, we took on through Sara from industrial poultry farms. They symbolised the vulnerability and pulse of emotional death – or complete detachment – that trauma brings about. White animals were the choice for sacrifice in ancient British culture. I have heard farmers and others with immersive animals experience, repeatedly talk about, what I had noticed independently, the particular vulnerability of white animals.

First of all, I suppose, white is a visual quality. White creatures are just much easier to spot in the dusk, where most predators operate. But also, in the case of chickens anyway, there is a predilection of character – the white ones are notoriously flighty, disengaged and hard to tame – or in the case of white rescue hen hybrids, nervous and alienated.

I have really only ever lived alongside one tame white hen, and she, poor creature, had to tame herself. A young cockerel she had raised from an egg (though she was not his biological mother, the fertile egg had been given to us) perhaps because he believed her the only genetically linked bird and therefore an inappropriate mate, pecked her almost to death when she came close. After a miserable period in the fox-and-badger-rich wood that took Pippi Longstocking, she returned to the grain feeder in the yard to eat and the cockerel attacked her. We found her, literally, at our doorstep with her head ripped to her skull and bleeding. We doused the wound and bone with TCP (writing this recalls the reek of that night) and put her in a box of hay, not expecting her to survive the night. She was bright the next morning. And so pliant and ready to be lifted and talked to, the opposite almost, in responsive noises afterwards, that we let her live alone in our plant garden, quietly digging up the bulbs and dislodging gravel, so that she recovered completely, scaly red skin knitting over her bare head. She even took a young cockerel love. They were an intense, inseparable pair, he an explosion of supple feathers, following her away from the flock, half her son. She, battered and inexpressive, with red shiny scarring instead of a helmet. Until a fox came into the fenced and dog guarded front garden and took her, also, one night.

So the chickens in their white silence, their blankness, represented for me, in a world dangerously displaced from language (a dark wood full of predators!) the work of mourning. Also, in the perceived smallness, muddiness and ridiculousness of my attachments; my inability to explain them to my Oxford spirit friends roaring towards the world, with minds ideal and conceptual, they provided, from them, from everyone, a kind of wall. Literally of flesh and feather. I think that wall protected me, and absorbed me, from a world in which, with a mind frozen in fear and unable through shock to process language, I was poorly equipped to deal.

One morning a dog rushed in at our gate and killed a white chicken. I wrote this poem, which marks for me the white space of forgetting in language. The wrench in the lines falls with the wrench in the chicken's throat.

WHITE CHICKEN

It has been a hard end of winter.
Everything frozen tight, and the
car welded to the track with black
ice, lethal under sole.

The snow still grazing the hill like sheep
the morning a dog killed our white
chicken. I left the gate open, from the car
tossed care to luck…*surely*
a white chicken can survive two hours?

Always — it's the white ones!

The copper hen, barrelling up; black, flame
tunnel of question – what happened, what
happened to her?

She has become snow.

She has drifted over the beehive, over the
camellia, she has fallen, scattered over the
sticks. There, where the dog caught her,
between the hedge and the drop, he broke her
neck. The shock of her dead, hangs,
abstract, out of reach. Absurdly flat,
neck twisted back. Her eyes are also now white.
We beat her down with a rake. Bury her
in a towel. The minnow daffodils and
irises push up under soft ghost leaves, the
snow of her is everywhere in the garden, it will not melt.
It will not melt with the season.

4. BLIND GUIDE

This section is named after one of our most memorable chickens, and one of the few who died of old age; though I wrote the poem when she was still alive.

She was a vast hen. Big and round and iron grey. A cannon ball. Quite humourless, or rather not friendly to humans, but probably because of her size, the most powerful member of the flock. First at the food and noisy. Pecking the younger and slighter if they were out of line. The boss.

I suppose I noticed her particularly because one of the effects of being knocked out of language, of shock, is that, partly for obvious reasons, you look to or need guides or leaders, bosses, in a different, more urgent way.

Without reflection or intention, after my sister's death, I subconsciously attached myself to powerful women, striking, articulate and capable, who would direct me in the new, unattached, space of mourning. In my head, which was still profoundly faith-driven in its structure, from my upbringing, I created a trinity of literal guides, whose words very simply, even at the points of greatest alienation, I could still hear. Women loud and clear in their kindness, who also made me long to speak.

This was not, I see now, in retrospect, an unproblematic flight of attachment from my missing home. For the women, who had mostly evolved their lead position through psychological hardship and extremity. For those already in their flock, who perceived me as an emotional threat. And for my own mental health, since like all attachment disorders, or flights from the murky mud yard of our humanity, it promised shining worlds it could not deliver.

Also the nature of subjugation to such a leadership is a kind of abjection, which as you recover, leads to a profound surge of negative or alienated feeling towards the one who dominates, who seems to control what should be autonomous.

Be that as it may, the big chicken was a leader in size, presence and voice.

The downside of holding such a position is that when death comes, in this case from the sky, she was the one who turned on it.

I heard what happened from the kitchen. Raucous, cacophonic squawking. Totally different in volume and mess from the sounds hens make, melodious, repetitive, when they have laid an egg.

I *think* when I went out to investigate, I saw something dark flap off into the sky. I may have imagined it, later. The hen herself had disappeared. I may have looked in and recognised her shape in the coop.

She did not come out. Not that day or the next. I thought she must have died but when I peered in, there she was, a massive dark shape. The other hens were confused and then found gentler, more fragmented ways to regroup. We left food and drink inside the coop for her.

It was our neighbour who told me that it is quite common for crows around where we live to dive bomb chickens (and lambs) and peck out their eyes. If anyone had rushed to the defence of the flock it would have been her. I *think* they got her.

She sat in the coop for three months. We thought she would probably die as chickens often do, from shock.

She did not die. To our amazement, she finally *emerged*, a bit less large and no longer the dominant chicken because she had lost her sight.

She had not actually lost her eyes, but they looked somewhat filmy.

'How do you *know* she's blinded?' asked the same friend who asked me why I spent so much time with chickens.

It was a good question. For a moment my mind guttered, thinking I had made the leader a pro-jection of my own terror, clinging to the pen because its eyes were out. But then, the answer when I thought about it was simple, 'Because she bumps into things'.

Much later, when we had penned the chickens against a bay window, I saw the blind chicken lower her head and use her red fleshy coxcomb, which looks a bit like a red bulbous washing up glove, to feel her way round the curve of the window – *as if it were a hand.*

Her fate fascinated me. Two of the three wom-
en guides who reached me at that moment of
explosion, event, whose voices were loud, clear,
central enough to be audible in the eye of death,
later had psychotic break downs, both associat-
ed with trauma when young. The events that
gave them the power and the courage to lead
and reach me, also at some point in their lives
swooped down on them and took them from,
changed their position within, the flock. For
me, who did not only love them, but who had
in fact imprinted on them, in absolute bond, at
that time of absolute disintegration of primal
identity (the re-breaking of the first trauma,
birth) this led, though it was many years later,
to real, startling sadness, tears of grief and be-
wilderment. I still feel the deepest emotional
gratitude to the guides who reached me, who
risked blindness in the scale or range of their
seeing, because of the way they faced death.

I drew two comforts from what happened to
the Blind Guide, who shuffled out again three
months later, in the tradition of Oedipus, Tire-

sias, Odin (and those literary guides, Milton, Joyce, where the pen (or key) had to be driven by the hand). And the chicken is the symbol of the thinker, the one whose hand seems firmly attached to its head. Firstly, she was never bullied by the other hens despite her disability. Secondly, she survived longer than any of them, protected from every fox attack and adventure out, by her disabled caution and proximity to the coop.

But what can I say about the fact she also draws, this guide, on other less positive, or more complex figures? The Pharisees, for example,'Woe to you... you make a single convert twice as much a child of hell as yourselves. Woe to you, blind guides...You blind fools...'

These leaders who crossed sea and land to reach me and then went mad (to convert me to their divine madness?) perhaps also did increase the hellishness, my acute sense of my own separated life negated through tragedy, the reality of it, squandered on poultry. Paltry things. But I also feel in my heart, that were that so, if they were indeed Christ's hypocrites driven by their own deaths, whited sepulchres, the mental blinding they suffered, re-authenticated them. Since it showed, so very clearly, how their behaviour was not personal; it was also grounded in personal tragedy, a grief event, that they also, in some ways, like me, had not had the space to mourn.

If not a hypocrisy or hubris, there is, at the very least, a paradox that lies at the heart of all true teaching and guiding, the love it evokes and its crashing central absurdity. As Jane Austen observed in high irony, nothing worth learning can be taught.

In this sense, the chicken guide's blinding, public and loud (it reached me through glass and brick inside the house!) was the awful crowning of her effectiveness as a guide or teacher (she used her crown as guide afterwards).

Anyway this blind guide (*hodegoi typhloi* in
Greek sounds, does it not, very similar to the
noise a chicken makes?) died of old age at about
six, big and round and heavy deep in her own
coop. She was always bad tempered after her
event. This is her poem.

BLIND GUIDE

So, long ago now… she was actually
the boss, big enough to peck
down every head, friendly –
but not entirely – mainly big.

Death

sounded like her crazed screech for life.
She fought it like she fought for the whole tribe,
I only dreamed its black flap up into the tree.
The caws.

Days she lay low in the coop,

days would not rise, then she came down so
sore and slow; so empty – and without her eyes.
Humiliating week to week – forgetting

power, living sightless fall – the others
did not peck her lower.

                    Sometimes though she
sat on them at night. Claw to eye.

                                By day,
she seemed content the longest time – a life –
to stand out in the air and let the sun burn
off her mites.

                  Then, at last, she laid an egg –
the colour and the feel of cool plaster.

                               After,
head lowered, at the border of her pen, she used
her flopped red crown to feel her way,
like a disarticulated hand.

                  Now, quiet queen, a little
light's returned, she bends to shape.

    I think she may live longest of them all.
So strong she is, so careful of herself.

5. OF CHICKENS AND HUMANS

The interspace between human beings and other animals, indeed between humans and the environment, is potential space. As human beings, we, or I, yearn to transcend our body and in one sense, through attachment, or at least through all the entanglements of connection, we do so – partially. Only once in my life have I had a curious, calm, completely immanent experience of body transference. As a young woman. I still don't know what to make of it. I was in a queue, looking at the back of a woman in front of me in a yellow sundress and I quietly had the strangest feeling from the inside and without strain how it felt to belong to that body; within it, each hair and freckle, equal and relaxed, as if I were in myself, I felt I was looking at my body that was hers. A friend of mine's daughter has said she has experienced something similar once – a sort of curious, memorable, sentient transmigration. I sometimes wonder if, unencumbered by language, that connection is what animals feel.

I certainly felt glimpses of it with my sister, and I think she must have too, as she wrote poems which my mother gave me after she died, about our bond, saying it was because we had been confined in one womb (a womb terrified of trapped birds, of dead creatures, of lightning). What I do remember is sometimes being floored by a gesture because it was so close to mine. Her boyfriend shrieking as I ambled out of her room in my dressing gown, 'You've got Flora's feet!'

Most of the time I have to imagine, feel, animals partially. In this world where the old transcendences are forbidden, many people have reversed God and seek him in Dog, looking in that most responsive of co-evolved minds for patterns of behaviour, that connect up below the canker – as it can seem – of information based language.

Clearly that reversal has driven me towards chickens. I see my being drawn to their quasi-reptilian, avian – un-mammalian anyway – qualities (they don't respond to touch so well, have a more separated relationship to their chicks, as egg layers, without those multiple milk portals out of the body, teats) they belong also to another medium, air.

I think in disaster, when emotion can be un-manageable and also unplaceable (the ground where it might be possible to feel has gone) we seek out radical others, as what Eliot might call 'objective correlatives' or emotional sumps. In my case, birds. In fact, as already implied, I observe a strange volatility in disaster, akin to the experience in the queue, but prolonged and in the mind, a sense of disassociation from the body and vanishing into the other. Shock de-magnetises identity (itself,

in part, cast through the trauma of birth) imprinting the person who lives it, shockingly,
lastingly, with the images and people who
were present within and around the crisis. It is
in part, for this reason I think, traumatised or
abused animals, as well as humans, repeatedly
put themselves in a position where they have
to be rescued again – in an attempt to reset the
dislocated, broken or demagnetised bond. To
reboot.

Under this, the yearning towards the 'animal
which therefore I am', the search for continuity, the maternal body from which I have been
blasted, is always a double bind with who/
whatever I search in. My dog, a king shepherd,
can feel like he's constantly searching my language, the cadence of spoken sentence structure, to enter it. I can say to him simply, in
words, I'm sorry you can't come with me today,
he shrugs and walks back to his bed. These days
he hardly wants to associate with other dogs,
would, I think be puzzled and affronted on the

level of species, if we took in another dog, so set he seems on transcending his being. He has taken to holding long conversations with us in the form of extended modulated groans. I think with him, of Buddhist stories of reincarnation; sense him one slim, permeable skin-life away from human.

Mostly our chickens have been content to cluck out a chicken-identical space alongside us, in much the same way as a cat holds a cat-like space. However one or two have strained to reorientate their being closer, to transcend their avian bodies.

Several, in fact, turned to us out of trauma. The white chicken, pecked to the skull by one of the cockerels, although previously a flighty, lunatic rescue, changed I suppose in despair, in that disintegration of primal identity that is the blow to the head, and engaged in communicative noise exchange, touch, to hand feeding, to being held. Another, just seemed innately highly intelligent and inquisitive, a copper black hen who used to wait outside our kitchen door, for contact with us in the morning. Her innate yearning for the impossible, even disdain for her kind, fascinated me and led to this poem.

CHICKEN 2

This chicken is ridiculous!
It doesn't even think it is a chicken…
day after day, its beak taps on the
glass door, clucking, throatily, 'Let me in!
Let me in! I am a human being!' Struts
into our kitchen. Affronted by exile. Undistracted
by the fireworks of its own plumage and
the cold yellow dot of its unredeemed,
prehistoric eye. It tries the chair. The dresser. As if
the act of arrival – its flame feathers – could mollify
God's cellular judgement on its being. When
we lift it to our breasts and bear it like a baby
back to its coop – its feet claw up the empty air –
its small, erect head ruffles at the insult of return – to those
flop crowned goose bump gossips; those dossers in the dust!

The fascination, the yearning between human and animal, was dramatically represented for me, and for my brilliant friend who is afraid of feathers (she comes from a country where perhaps it has historically been more vital to recognise and manage, at all costs, the negative outward effects of terror) in a British Museum exhibition, focusing on the domestic paraphernalia of Pompeii, that disaster town. Amongst many nubile statues and lamps (in the shape of phalloi) one statue made us stop. We felt it the most fascinating in the exhibition. Pan making love to a goat, penetrating it from behind with a look of focused ecstasy on his face. This knot of complexity was, it seems, an acceptable, bourgeois garden ornament in ancient Italy. One to pick up, perhaps, at a Roman Dobbies.

(I am thinking suddenly of a cartoon sent yesterday of this recent disaster, pandemic, as a Pan-demic, with hundreds of Pans running around on goat hooves, and nymphs running...)

Derrida separates himself and his Cartesian tradition lightly from such a lusty commingling between us all – assessing the difference between human and animal as one of inflected thought – condensed in the experience of nakedness, his cat stares at him naked in the bathroom and he, the man, feels shame at the simplicity of, the 'just to see' nature, of the cat's stare. Others have argued different distinguishing marks between humans and other animals; face, *mourning*, hand (Heidegger makes the implicit association with writing) language, cooking ability, and intriguingly the gluteus maximus, the bottom, which uniquely allows us to run upright for extended lengths of time and therefore use complex tools in the hunt, spears, arrows, etc... As someone who has been fascinated by female social roles, I myself might well argue that we are one of a very small group of animals, who go through menopause half way through our lives. In fact the only primate (even chimpanzees menstruate until they are seventy...) and that our evolution and current position of power on the earth's surface is therefore the result of the wisdom of older women who can look up from the absorption and mortal danger of childbirth, 'the slough of fertility' for a few years to ground and direct the species towards corporate wisdom. I might.

So, I certainly think part of our yearning towards animals, and Derrida perceives the nexus of energy which he feels as shame, is the fact the cat is looking (impassively! Can you believe it?) at his naked sex. At a difference and link in sexual body, that is so strongly and – to my contemporary, English eye, not especially trained to swan rape, and cow coupling – shockingly – represented in the completely eclipsed, therefore remarkably preserved, trauma site of Pompeii. Where gods *need* to make love to animals. That is the centre of the connection. In chickens sexuality may be different again, very. The older cockerel will have what appears brutal sex with every hen in the flock, damaging the hen's heads with the beak and also her wings with his spurs. It seems as if he has a different usage of old and young chickens since, in our flock anyway, the older hens are invariably more used sexually and the younger hens more attached to the cockerel; the youngsters often follow and sleep alongside the cockerel. In return for his (dubious?) attention, the cockerel makes a show of strut or protection, which can be real and discerning, or cowardly pretense, depending on the character of the bird. He also makes an inviting, clucking noise around the food provided (by us, actually) and forebears to eat until the hens have eaten. The hens, in return, have busy sex with every available cockerel and store their sperm in the ovum for months to fertilise eggs as they are made. They have the amazing ability to retain multiple, different sperm supplies to use the highest quality sperm at the time of fertilisation. For me, caught in the terrible, sickly, slowing of time in trauma, the compressed sheet of time trickling back towards disaster, where lovers and friends rise and vanish, almost like symbols, without the emotional space for proper, human mourning; I mean really caught in the inability to feel; the numbness and emptiness that comes out of sudden loss; all models of sexual difference are strangely comforting and companionable.

The poem, which is laughing as much at my own presumptuous mental state as it is at the chicken. My attempts at pure thought. My numerous attempts at transcendence, knocking on the glass without much more real effectiveness than Woolf's dying moth knocks at the window. Knock, knock, knocking on heaven's door. So the flaming hero in these post, post modern days, or always, whose crown is a fleshy hand, the head hand, must be lifted and put back in the dust.

I actually really liked to come down and to find this hen had slipped in again to sample the fruit bowl, give the bread a try, or simply to stalk the floor. I was grateful too for the opportunity she gave me to play human, to exercise the law of the interior. Only her shit got to me.

Substandard bottom.

6. ON VIOLENCE

1

Fizzy died this week – our old cockerel –
(who I secretly called Kraken) –
Fizzy, eBay egg posted in polystyrene –
Fizzy – non-stop, non-stop chirping chick –
our grey hen sat wing-wrapped on the roof –
foreswearing broodiness – my son said –
'That chick thinks he's a prophet!' Habakkuk...
Fizzy. Big. Jet fat and white. Steaming up the
stone path. Strut. Stop. Down. Cockadoor!
Blocking the quiet sky.
Pecking the hens' heads to black blood. Fizzy.
Hypochondriacal, sick with thug-thwart, his neck
along my arm, mammoth, tragic-weight –
Fizzy banished to field compound behind
double barbed wire, his feeders armed with
water pistols, against attack; he and his
tough old, beak-hacked, clawless battery hen
who strutted and beat him up right back – Fizzy – gone.

This verse-note record of big, white, violent Fizzy – first and dread sign of the cockerel at our house – spans the five years of his life. Like many other big, bully males he lived a long and lucky life, dying of old age, a heart attack, in the door of his coop.

His coop was not at our house. We passed him on. He went to live in Sara's field with a battered battery hen, behind a two layered wall of barbed wire, like Hannibal Lecter. Even so, he attacked Lee, Sara's wife, when she carried in the mash, so that she learned to enter armed with a water pistol.

We expelled Fizzy slowly, agonisingly, because he was raised by us but also attacked every human in the yard, especially, but not exclusively, men. A full blown attack with claws. Hurling his impervious, blank, white weight at the back of the knees or at the eyes. For the first time, I felt I understood the carved stone cockerels representing the Fighting French at

Blenheim. When he was not fighting he was crowing loudly, on and on. Our neighbours at a Residents Meeting put him on the agenda and debated whether Fizzy's noise was a nuisance. We half hoped it was, so we could have an honourable reason for strangling him. While we waited for the verdict we put him in the cloakroom at night. So he split our dreams wide open, at five in the morning in the summer. The Residents Association kindly decided his sound was atmospherically rural, but when he was not crowing, he was attacking and raping hens, who had bleeding backs and torn heads. When he was not raping he was strutting, puffing out his feathers like a fan to the floor and chortling at, it seemed, his own gorgeousness. When he was not chortling, he was staging sickness. Lying in my arms, stretching his neck along them asking, apparently, in a profoundly needy, un-avian, way for sympathy. His was the complete *opposite* to hen behaviour. As our vet observed, at the bottom of the food chain hens tend habitually to play down their sickness.

Thus if a hen appears to be ill – shows symptoms – it is usually very sick indeed.

I had raised Fizzy since a chick and so we had a bond. He did not, usually, attack me. Even later in Sara's field he let me into his pen unarmed and fed from my hand. Perhaps I was just flattered that I had some power with him. I would like to think I valued his ability to discriminate. Certainly there was physical pleasure in feeling his weight on my arm, as there is in any animal that seems to have chosen you.

But letting go of him was more complicated. At the same time, I was grimly tangled with a man, my husband then, whom I realise now, I accepted with the detachment, almost indifference, of an obedient child. He had a kind manner and was good at handling horses. I remember literally thinking, 'O, he is just a man! Any man will do!' nor at the time did I have space in my hammering emergency mind, in trauma flight, to consider that this was not a desirable, or even usual, way to approach love and, ideally, life-long, commitment. That it might, in fact, derive rather from the stupor of trauma than from my own heart (Blake chose a wife after his brother's death, at once, in a similarly random way).

My mother, she who was so frightened of trapped birds, dead creatures, storms and whom I knew I loved, wanted me to marry. I wanted to please her, whose own husband seemed to us fantastically cruel. Here was someone attractive enough, about the right age, who wanted me. Only my body, in fact, rebelled – as if it knew – archived in it somewhere – more – *more* – could be possible. It was, of course, the throat, the lungs that took it. (Nicole Loraux, notes that in classical Greek drama, whilst men die through all sorts of injuries; kidney, heart, liver, side etc; women die through the throat – the voice – whether scarf, rope, knife, removal of air...) I had a throat infection, coughing, turning to pneumonia, broke a rib coughing, meaning that not my large, home wedding, but, my hen party, that festivity of communally deactivated terror, had to be called off.

Anyhow, I could have been lucky with my gamble. I wasn't, particularly. I married a man who though not violent found other subtler ways to control. He ran up debt on many credit cards and persuaded me to pay them off. Again, again and again. He wouldn't pay for anything communal. Sensing, I think, both trauma and perhaps profounder inequalities, he milked me again and again for whatever money I would give him – and when my parents passed on a share of compensation payment for my sister's death, that became, briefly, quite a lot. In the end, staring my mother's very clear and directive Christianity in the face, I tried to separate financially, legally, from him just to keep afloat with the children (since I was frozen from feeling, logically, it made sense to obey my mother). I found an arcane legal structure called Judicial Separation. It never occurred to me that how I felt for this man (blank), despite the loving conception of our children, was the deeper key to our incompatibility. Or that there was anything other than pure principle in my mother's injunction (and I am grateful to Bernadine Evaristo for her work exploring the taboo of mother, son-in-law passion). Or even, that really someone who cared so little for how I felt about his behaviour, was unlikely ever to make a good companion.

No matter. I now had two babies, whom I loved in the deepest mammalian complicity and to the whiteness of the sky (though I did not know then, how far they would turn our meeting around). I loved being with them; had largely given up work to look after them. Later, really, I realised that my husband's conduct was not so much to do with my situation or even me, though he was good, I think, at spotting potential vulnerability. If anything, it seemed grounded rather in his own need to run his life on the edge of risk – to replay the beauty and re-

lief of life's randomness for his singular thrill,
again and again and again – a position with
which I partially empathised because it was itself the result of trauma; his army parents sent
him away at six to boarding school for terms at
a time and...

Anyway, the point here is that my relationship
with this man made the experience of wilful
boundary making with a violent cockerel more
complex, and, at the time, I wrote this second
verse note, in the Fizzy poem, which almost
makes me laugh now,

2
Charlie, filed for Decree Absolute –
we got divorced – this week. Charles (I call
him now) forgot this final step. We had put
up a fence, judicial separation – he,
robbed of what (on earth!) to grab – strutted
up and down, crowing at the quiet sky
Look at my white belly! Cockawawk!
He grew up here... we allowed him –

this – whole years swallowed up
in growing strut, red bubbled air.
If contact's needed now – we go in armed –
hold his self pity, carefully, away,
feel, take care to name the maculate
world outside his grip; fear
for the girl he holds down now. What
will Charlie take from her? How long for her
to name the quiet clouds? To step
from what will not stop for gentleness? Charlie. Gone.

Reading this poem now reminds me of the terrible sense of entwinement or bond, of loveless connection, within which my ex-husband and I both twisted, for years. Charlie did not 'remember' to file the final papers for decree absolute. We were not, though I only found this out by chance when I applied for a visa, formally separate for years afterwards.

I had the deepest sense that my husband grew up, developed his pattern of behaviour, in relationship with me, though I met him in his thirties. That I was therefore in a sense responsible for it. I used the money I had saved to train him to be a lawyer late in life as if I wanted to enable him to stay entangled. He, no doubt, used my uncertainty. But I did too. To keep myself from re-entering a world of bigger loss, of explosion. Significantly, I felt that if at any time, my husband had admitted he had a problem with money, expressed contrition for the suffering he was causing (at times I could not pay for our food) and made moves towards change, I would have stayed with him. However he became increasingly unpleasant and demeaning, seeking in my humiliation the space he needed away from his own behaviour. Repeatedly in fact he called me, 'Foul'. Fowl. Eliding me with my terror.

By making a distance from him, moving out, with the help of friends and also the teacher I trusted, I found that, to my own surprise, far from being destroyed (which I decided by that stage, I would rather be, than submit to the endless puffery and crowing) I felt a great deal better.

Our marriage ended, literally, with a game of 'chicken' – or that's what we used to call that game boys in Birmingham in the 1980s used to play – running at each other or, later, driving cars straight at each other to see who would swerve first. Charlie, who was frightened his behaviour would compromise his career, said he would sue for half the house I had bought with Flora's money, unless I promised to sign a Gagging Order, legally promising to tell no one what he had done. I thought deeply and with a dark mental shift of gear, let the house go, deciding I would rather lose the house than my voice. So I said, I won't be gagged – go for the house. He did not. Maybe because he realised if he took us to court, what he most feared would certainly happen. He swerved.

It took me years to move away from his properly snarled up masculinity and, some of, my own delusions about love. As part of that process and because I found it so difficult to stand up in court and bear witness, I trained and worked to support court witnesses. In one, memorable, training session, the instructor, who was inspired, showed us on a slide various types or models of domestic abusers. One type, Model 4, corresponded to Charlie exactly. The trainer described the kind of target Model 4, would choose; a woman, solvent, with a reasonable job and her own property, but with some kind of trauma in their past that would make them easier to sever, vulnerable. Someone who had seen the black lines between things and lavished affection on chickens. In short, so it felt, me. It was the first time I had considered the very serious effect my own fear, was having on my life.

I still remember very clearly the shock of that training session. I sat in a kind of trance, unable to join in, as five years of what had felt like uniquely mysterious, personal suffering, the drama of my name itself, already played out in the media, became a lino cut, that simply made a pattern. Over and over and over and over and over and over and over again. I conformed to a type. He conformed to a type.

The experience connects with my need to watch the paltry poultry, the foul fowl, to see in their quiet, profound, anonymous bodies, the patterns of closest connection of which trauma had robbed me. And with my desire to write it, to make or show poetry as a transferrable model.

Also at that time, I began in poetry and in my mind, to extend the pattern, initiated in Fizzy, outwards. So, at the same time as Fizzy's death and Charlie's divorce, politically, Mugabe fell from power in Zimbabwe. This felt particularly connected because one of the neighbouring families who were particularly supportive during divorce, 'Think of him as a rhino, Cathy, beautiful out in the bush but not right in the compound, in your house...' were refugees really from Zimbabwe. They had lost close family members in brutal murder and their livelihoods in their home country, but considered themselves lucky in the context of the many black lives that simply vanished (or reappeared as dead numbers to support the regime).

3

Mugabe stopped being president
of Zimbabwe this week. He did not stop
at raising ghosts from dead electoral lists
to vote himself the best. He did
not stop at torture. Mugabe took
every other voice – on paper,
radio and news – that did not cock
his hoop. He stopped it dead.
He made heads bleed all right. Mugabe
let the farms die empty – and he
stopped the grain, and school,
and all the play of sexuality. He
killed the animals and upped his
shopping wife. Mugabe broke

the work of de-colonialism, blocked
the subtle thought of shady, moving minds,
coding black and white as absolutes. He
downed his friends. Mugabe. Gone.

Fizzy. Charlie. Mugabe. It is possible to extrap-
olate the big from the small.

I cannot see the other way round.

Re-reading this now, something returns about
the roots of domestic abuse. I felt such a frus-
tration when my daughter, at eight, insisted
on calling the loud peeping chick, Fizzy. Although the name went with her high pony tail
and years. (I had a similar internal war with my
Mum at eight, wanting to call our pale labrador
puppy Toffee, which I thought was the most
perfect name, while she wanted to call her Can-
dida, the Latin for white.)

Perhaps, because I remembered the feeling of
being overwhelmed by my mother's sureness,

perhaps because I thought *it is only a chicken*, I let my daughter win the name-game with Fizzy.

But I also named the chick in my heart, looking at it, with my mother's clarity, *Kraken*. I sometimes still have visions of the secret soul-names of things (including my own daughter's soul name) and I felt the chick was, secretly, Kraken. Partly because it was the only one of six incubated eggs at that time successfully to crack out of its shell. Partly because there was something, from the beginning, unstoppable and therefore seemingly monstrous, in his noise. More than the astonishing, precocial aptitude of every new hatched chick.

I think my son sensed it, too. I remember looking with him, at the chick and at the reaction of the adult hens, who literally used to hide from the incessant peeping, up high, wings over the head. That paradoxical fight, the 'War on Terror', also of course, the War of Terror, was raging at the time and young people and their

teachers were primed to Look Out for Extrem-
ism. 'He is like a mad prophet', my son said.
And he was. Peep-peep-preaching to his mother. To all the hens. To us. All the time. Nonstop.

At a similar time, my son, who was very small,
wanted to use my family surname, as I was
bringing him up and liaising, and funding
school. His father, who had already taken a
great deal of money from my family, then took
me to court, not to gain more access to his children (which is what I feared) but for allowing
my son to use my name at school. So reasonable, so I thought, that my son should use the
name I use, given his father neither lived with
nor provided for his children and I was making their care my life, that I went into court
without representation, despite my husband's
career and familiarity with the legal system.
I will never forget the experience. The judge
after chatting about the firm my ex-husband
worked with, asked him very gently why he
was not paying for anything, and explained to

me, with a smile, that my son was a little too young to decide to take the name of the woman who physically bore him, was raising him and also sheltering, feeding and housing him. That in fact, the (dishonest and casually abusive) man I had been married to who shared the judge's occupation, had that right. The name was, by law, the father's right. He went on, if I remember rightly, to talk about his cow herd.

The judge's calmly delivered calumny simply burned me like fire. I could not believe or feel that this law of the name was justice. At the same time as I found myself loving and funding two children who bore the name of the man who was defrauding us, my ex-husband used in all correspondence a diminishing 'sweet' pet name, that he had not in fact really used when we were together as an improbable couple, 'Cathy-Cath'. The combination of his legal action to occlude my name and the diminution of my first name in address, was central to the damage my ex-husband wanted, or felt

entitled now that I refused his, rather singular, 'attachment', to inflict on me. Therefore of
course, with deep enough thought, it was also
the key to what I needed. In the name, in the
irreducible singularity of the signature, lay –
for absolute certain – my survival. There is a
fourth verse to the Fizzy poem I forgot that I
also wrote:

4
This Sunday morning, thinking
of the name – of shifts –
of the block print of violence –
how it lifts. How it comes down and
down upon the world, both different
and the same, like
some roll of thin Soviet
waxed paper – or some sleek Cole-
fax wall – and how that quiet
thought does down the splintering of
mind that disrupts the pattern.

An attempt, that I lived through to the point
of madness almost, to disrupt the 'brute boot

on the human face forever'. To refuse, against my strongly Christian mother's absolute injunction, to allow someone's truly toxic masculinity to continue centrally in our lives simply because mine had been smashed (of course it is still in our lives but less). A forced revolution of the death-frozen heart. The reference in the verse, to Soviet wrapping paper, reminds me of seeing, with a Russian friend, examples of printed wrapping in an exhibition about domestic display in the Russian Revolution and feeling the strength, the intensity of her emotion going round, as if her heart still carried the grief of that collective violence, permeating, in-erasable. It is this struggle that, as I have written, I also saw as the work of poetry, though now I think that is just one aspect. I believe I learned that patterned seeing, profound, emergent, and monstrous, from the skill of my teacher herself a survivor of abuse, who now Instagrams her photo with one eye concealed by her black dog...

No,
thinking of pattern – the poem
that can hold the page and that defies
the page – showdown of unbeing,
to the monster. Half strangled,
dimensionally transformed.
stripped of skin, emerging,
different to itself, tamed,
one eye open,
still alive – still here.

I would note one further aspect of Fizzy-
the-Cockerel's violent, sociopathic character. *He came by post.* A stowaway into our lives
through death's dream of the circulation of
pure language, separated writing. I bought
fertile eggs on eBay, for our hopelessly broody
hen, and they arrived in a jiffy bag, packed up
in polystyrene. The one that survived this most
detached and clinical of beginnings was 'Fizzy'.
I do sense an echo with 'Charlie' sent away to
boarding school at six, insentient by training,
ripped up from primal attachment, imported
by me to please my parents.

Finally I want to report, very clearly, that I felt nothing when Fizzy died. A half laugh and sigh in my throat at Sara's text, *'he was a character'*. Our 'attachment' was purely physical. Also, that I came away from the experience of living with him, believing all cockerels to be psychopathically violent. I have had partially to relearn cockerels, through raising and bonding with different ones, Susan (who seemed gender fluid for a long time, perhaps because we wanted hens so much) and Lokhi, father and son, the colour of ash and flame. Many cockerels, it turns out, are capable both of cheerful brotherly friendship, of contributing to harmony within a group and of affectionate, bonded coexistence with hens. Learning this for me has been a difficult journey. Nor do I underestimate the one that my children face.

7. MOTHERHOOD

When we talk about death in its fullest meaning, it always appears a double death. The death of the beloved and it seems myself.

My mother said to me, when I was a child, 'If something happens to any of you, that will be the end of me.'

Something happened.

A sense – at that time when my sister was blown up – in the bone white shield/screen of adrenaline – that there was a black line round things. That, motherless, the world was separated. No connection between things. No word.

I did not understand at the time that my mother's emotional disappearance was part of her mourning and mine. I *certainly* did not have the depth of experience to understand that participation in political culture may require, as Morrison deftly shows, the work of double death of the beloved.

Motherhood works at the heart of my studies on chickens, its fears and shadowing. Motherhood, as it was represented to me as a child. The greatest energy. The biggest sacrifice. My mother's story was one of motherlessness – her desire to undo that lack in her mothering of us – her lovely passion. So her sudden emotional vanishing was difficult for us.

But in her own heart, I suppose, familiar.

I spent years, in my studies, searching for mothers to move through after she had vanished. I wrote an undergraduate thesis on Julian of Norwich who imagines God as mother and I observed people who were skilled at mothering themselves, without another.

Obviously the way that chickens mother is radically different from human mothering. They are not mammals – but no one who has handled a broody hen could question the strength of the bond. I have been fascinated through observing artificial incubation, as well as chicks hatched by hens, to watch the avian process of imprinting (with all its textual resonance, including my need to write this piece) followed by the gradual integration of chicks within the flock – the aggression between older hens and chicks, mild if conditions are halcyon, softening in co-raising – and the bonds that form and flake between youngsters – as they find a way to enter the flock and separate from the mother.

As I have kept chickens, I have also been a mother myself. Without my sister. She wanted to be a mother very much, and promised she would look after my children. In one sense I have had to keep asking myself again and again, framing and re-framing, how to be a good mother. How to spring my children's spirits?

It is the simple, safe answer to my friend's question, 'Why do you spend so much time with chickens?', 'I am trying, in sometimes difficult circumstances, to create the quiet, consistent space where my children can grow.'

The following poem, written half a decade ago, touches on the despair, fear, latent in the invisible, alchemical work of motherhood. Work that in one sense, in my observation of children, is the most valuable, and undervalued (hard to value because if it is successful its signed traces evaporate) – and because, when I was young anyway, it was considered a sort of sell-out, a sentimental nostalgia against the more overt political values and raw career ambition of separated female agents, upheld by college and school.

The tension between those values and my deep, as it turned out, not completely reactionary, instinct to stay mum, to give motherhood primacy, held within it the most sustained, immanent happiness I have experienced in my life, when my children were young, and pride in them now (am I beginning to sound like an eighteenth century tomb stone?). Also to the trace of despair – the foregoing of my dreams and longing for a very different identity which might have been made possible by my sister's life – and this poem.

I remember, I showed this poem at the time I wrote it to an old friend of mine, from a similar background, in a similar position as a mother, and it haunted her. The hen which it describes, came from outside, a livestock show, as if there were a link between its genesis and its symbolic extremity...

MOTHER

The image of this hen will disappear soon.
She came in a card box, and sat an evening
While we had tea, on the kitchen island,
Beside her speckled sister; wide eyed, blinking.

Of the two, she was the brighter one.
Released, she explored the pen in feathered snow
Shoes, strutting over the fissures in the bark,
While her sister sat.

She became the communicator. The one who moved
Between the flock and the sister who sat;
Who, while she pecked at the dust with the lead hens;
Returned to the one who was afraid.

Then she laid eggs. I looked in that first day
And thought her dead. She was so flat and her
Throat lolled strangely. I took the top off and,
Seeing that she lived, quietly we replaced

The dud laid eggs with potential ones.
And waited. She sat differently from other hens,

Not like a flat iron hissing; wholly slumped, her gaze entranced;
A catholic saint in ecstasy; I do think some Virgin

Shape; some ghost ideal of mother killed her.
Thirty days without water or food.

In the end we grabbed her. Forced a grain solution
By syringe, into her gullet. She just sat.
The food lay in the beak. She, who had
Shouted out so loud when young allowed us all to touch.

At the end, lifting her off her eggs, was like
Lifting dry wood. She was buried, but could have
Easily been tossed up in the air, or in a pile
Of leaves. The difference between real death
And her maternal trance was very quiet.

For a while, we considered the eggs.
They may have had life inside, but that *barrier*
Between the shell and all of us, the smooth quiet
Shell prevented our connection. What good

Is life that's so invisible? What good was hers,
That killed what she loved most?

The poem apart from holding the secret fear of the work of motherhood itself, the murder of the beloved, also contains simply the terrible fear that one's most destructive or sabotaging patterns are passed on to the destruction of one's child – one of the agonies of parenthood. It also puts lines round the central work of mourning, with which I began. We cannot escape the fact that we die with the dead, with our children. Julian of Norwich prays for protection from the double death, mother and child, figure of eight, at the heart of fear. Though I do not think we can escape from it, we can also emerge...

Having watched imprinting and given birth myself, I recognise the gap between the child and me, by my sense of the offspring's spirit, Pippi's quiet intelligence, our newly hatched young hen, Bluey's, gentleness, my daughter's scrutinising independence. Also by the trauma of their emergence; birth, hatching in which the young freeze on, follow, the one who bore

them, take in and internalise their characteristics, embedded in their appearance and
language. Burn it into their brain receptors. I
think this latter, this imprinted trace is what
we superficially understand by character.

And it is this imprinted trace that is in a sense
undone by later trauma. The strength of the explosion, of shock, of sudden death. The aware-
ness, I remember the words inside my own
head, 'nothing is going to be the same again'.
In that hour, which is like death itself, in which
everything separates, as if it had a child's black
line around it, character is de-magnetised and
you perhaps imprint on those around you
then, in my case friends and teachers, in an ab-
surd way, as if they were family, the ones you
must die not to lose. To an extent, I think that
shift of identity happens to all of us in the explosion of growing up, but we become, if that
coincides with trauma, as it did for me, Trauma's Babies, the children of the bone white
present, those Doris Lessing calls the 'Children

of Violence'. Un-mothered by death. Imprinted on loss. Lost and in a stupor (Stupa). Better that rupture, than entrapment in the ideal states of the frozen family, a bark light mother. To be an egg abandoned in the shell...

8. ON THEFT

Just as the one who lives with her children alongside chickens, nurturing her latency, can feel alienated from the world of other work; so the busy, efficient, separated one may long for the trance of motherhood – the one who will also die.

Egg theft is easier for birds clearly than baby theft for primates. Eggs are such discrete, silent, rollable objects...

In a David Attenborough programme, that imprinted on my mind, a high caste orangutan (according to the over-narrative) long, important, ginger-armed, childless, swung down and snatched an orangutan baby from the arms of its mother. I remember the distress calls, the screaming, very clearly.

Interesting then that my actual memory of witnessing child theft is filmic, not real, a narrative or paranoia engendered by death's mad, imaginary eye. Theft may be an affect of art but not of life. A game of pure simulacra. I have felt it as terror very deeply, woken weeping with it, having seen my own mother and sister vanish. Yet here in the yard, by where I live, I have seen chicks share hens, and hens incubate other hens' eggs, I have seen cockerels attack chicks but I have never seen a hen steal another chick. I think, because of imprinting, it may at the deepest level, be impossible to steal. In its full legal meaning, to permanently deprive. I recognise very closely the fear Pullman evokes, of the Gobblers taking live children to the Frozen North to have their energy extracted. I feel also like I know that North. Have lost so much time, half a lifetime, learning to survive in it – but the ice is not the centre – the extreme at the end of the emotional compass. The North is pure terror. And it is the counter sign of home.

And we humans steal eggs from the chickens most days. It is why we separated them from other birds and brought them into us; their ability to lay all year round, itself a response to the variable timings of bamboo seed release. No wonder, given this theft, that a chicken's primary instinct is fear and that, as we established at the beginning, this is what their species' name has come to mean with us. Our hands, symbols of our human-ness, like fleshy spiders, creeping into the dark of the chicken coop and closing round them. Every day. Animated spectres of the fleshy crowns on their heads (apparently the thing that attracts chickens to each other).

Yet we, or I, am angry, at the brute thuggery of any other creature, a magpie for example, who comes and smashes an egg of mine – which it will, if you leave an egg outside on the table, even for a minute.

And so proud and self righteous to rescue a bird from a farming atrocity. (For I think whoever lives alongside chickens senses the fact that billions of chickens are raised in factories without natural light or room to move or to live out any of their subtler characteristics before slaughter is horror. The shame of our age. No less, for example, than child chimney sweeping in London, for the eighteenth century.) We have had a horror-shop of chickens over the years. Lasered beaks. Ammonia blind eyes. Knobbled feet. Vitamin E deficient flopped neck. Strung ham strings – birds walking with a Nazi rather than avian goose step.

And feel a cleaner propriety in our spirits as the wounded one gradually grows sleeker, brighter eyed, rediscovers the borders of her first imprint, her character. Until, suddenly, most of them, all except the blind one and the cockerels, are lost to the woods, or a fox, or a dog, or something that climbed the trees. Cull. Cull. Cull.

Are we good? Or bandits of fantasy, using their mute forms as partial, un-reciprocal buffers against our own terrified insentience?

Like the worst kind of writers, film makers, liberal thinkers.

Like those I despise, like I am.

It must be a very deep instinct in a chicken to gather her own eggs into a clutch, a dozen, like these chapters. And chickens are very instinctual creatures. Perhaps they feel something like I do when I write these words, that I am following a line that has already been written, filling ghost meaning with words.

Interestingly, the first poem I wrote about egg theft, a couple of years ago, was not about chickens. I repeat, I observe chickens are fairly relaxed about whose eggs they are sitting on. Rescue hens will drop out their eggs, unconcerned, bald and alone, on the yard concrete. I have several times hatched eggs under a bird who is not the genetic mother; if present for incubation she will still behave with maternal accuracy.

This poem then is about penguin egg theft; the response to another film clip from the Arctic shown in a wildlife programme which brilliantly, in its narration, touched my own terror. It showed the preternatural struggle across the ice penguins make to feed their young – and their bafflement and grief – expressed in the bend of the neck, the shuffle, when an egg is knocked away by another, eggless bird – usually to the egg's destruction because of the risk of instant freezing away from belly warmth.

The first film had strong resonance for me, primarily because of the stance of the mother and the fate of the egg, the baffled wastage of both, but also because of the ice – a strong current metaphor for textuality – the infinitely refractive wildness where nothing can grow, in which Dr Frankenstein is ultimately trapped with his monster – the space of pure terror, of spirit, that Heidegger will not chronicle, where my own many mother-daughter spirit guide adoptions fuse – in the sudden evaporation of bond in trauma – the recognition of the mortal separation between things – a crystallised learning space of pure adrenaline that seems to offer a bone white heaven but that in reality separates me from life's shadow cave, at the static pole of being. The landscape of art.

HARD POEM

Sometimes penguins' eggs are smashed –
won't lay – or else the eggs are not moon hard
– like soft spiders' eggs – a membrane
sack of milky sun the air can freeze.

Air and ice between their legs… sans flight…
these penguins are obsessed with pearls.
Nacreous pearls, identical, perfect
for the milky sunset of the pouch – no further detail

of the zygotic alphabet that makes an egg become.
(No pity either for the others' months of hunting
on the iridescent ice, the swallowing, swallowing
of globule, bone and shell!)

They see a pearl. They have a hook.
They roll the egg away... the mother
preens her lover's throat or stares up at green lights –
then she's bereft herself.

                Squatting on blackness

she often dies of grief. (As for the chicks –
they also rarely live.) How to grow
to one who dreamed a blank
for her desire? One who models theft?

9. THE LOST CHILD

I have written before about the tendency in the abject terror of sudden loss, to create idealised guide figures. Of my own creation of a trinity of real guides, two, the kindest, suffered psychotic episodes decades later – to relieve themselves, as it seems to me now, from the white space of separated trauma in which they met me so clearly and freely at the event.

My dozen eggs take a dark turn.

Certainly the emotional sterility of life on the ice has seemed to grow increasingly complex and painful for my spirit guides, for us all. And as things grew harder I found my guides had begun to perceive me, immobile but present, as very little more than a chicken myself. An embodiment of fear and failure to connect.

So, when my beautiful, strong, kind and raw daughter, became a teenager, they came, as it seemed, from the ice of my terror, these empowered, ice dextrous ones, to get her. I suppose my guides had despaired of me because I seemingly had achieved nothing visible in my silent struggle with death, and they thought they could rescue the most interesting, living part of me, my daughter, from the banality of our life and make something of her. As generations of flesh spiders have thought. From Rapunzel's sorceress, to Aunt March. In thinking this, they did indeed bring about change.

I did not show much emotional response when the world media crept over my own story and reported its most central bonds night after night, in the voyeuristic entertainment that passes among fools for news. I did not take my father's ghostwriters to task, when they fictionalised vital stages of all of our lives, to promote a hagiography. I did not show anger when my boyfriend in the tragedy, who had touched me with insentient hands, went on to make his name with a novel, rolling parts of the story away to his own artistic ends. I felt passive, helpless, in the face of these ethically despicable thefts – the easy blurring of the imaginary and real for aesthetic ends – the failure to mark the impossible difference between lost human life and our imagination that Primo Levi nails brilliantly in *The Drowned and The Saved*. I accepted their loose bandit flesh fingers in my box. As if I myself did not believe myself that I might still be alive, frozen in trauma's infinite present. As if, I repeat, I were a simulacra. As if my boyfriend's contention that I was dead, because I had left him, was true. I was reluctant to push my disgust and Levi's truth to its logical end, because it signalled the agony at the end of mourning – that though my sister was dead, I at some soily level, was not.

But the thieving nature of these spirit figures' approach to my child did enrage me. A border, I had forgotten I ever had, began to burn.

I repeat, down in the yard itself, I have not witnessed a hen steal a living chick, though I have seen them share. I was a mother. I turned. To the brightest, funniest mothers who lived around me, the local Mums of my children's friends, together we lifted the lid on the box and watched the scary flesh spiders scuttle in my head, but also, to be fair, outside it. It is hard to explain how. (Another wildlife film; wolves chasing bison, snapping at the heels of their tiring calves. At a point, as if with one thought, the bison stop running from the wolves. They stand. Make a circle around their young and butt the predators with the ring of their heads. The wolves, circle, tire and leave.) We made a ring of light and heat around the children. We kept them in our yard. It was an extraordinary time. Light comments, 'It is wrong to target children without you, separately', 'It puts the children in a very difficult and unnatural position to be suddenly subject to so much sudden attention' slid me further away from my spirit guides.

From a distance my guides it would seem really were snow blind. Since they were oblivious to the tiny, subtle, sinews of emotional connectivity that fed and shaped my daughter, made her loveliness and, as I thought, kept her safe. The perfect forms, who I had idealised so hard and high were not only powerful, competent, separated, they also were in part emotionally fractured.

Of course.

That's why they could meet me in the moment of trauma, of death, so clearly. No one, not even Heidegger could write that space, of appearing in vanishing – a space I sensed as pure fear – even when I was a child. I suppose my anger, for which read horror, for which read terror, was greater because I saw in their ghostly outreach now towards my daughter, a generation before, my own annihilation. Death had blown my family apart and these white-will minds, these creeping flesh spiders, these head-hands, these spirit mothers, these artists, these ghosts, had lifted me. Did they think I had learned nothing in all my life? I felt I at last understood, why the devil in Julian of Norwich's *Revelations of Love* is defined by his big hands. I was a lost child; my daughter, absence's child, a victim of nothing.

My mother had disappeared emotionally, once again, she always said she would if any one of us died, 'It will be the end of me'. My father, like my spirit friends, had been emotionally stripped out as a child, and seemed only able to operate on the white spirit plain, in the media flash light. Who was there to hold us, with messy corporate love, on the ground? That had been in part my sister's role. She and I literally spent hours in our teenage years, rolling on our parents' bed talking, talking, talking about who and where we were. Since she was killed there had been nobody I could talk to with such delicious, wild, taboo-less absolute freedom. For the spirit guides, like all the after figures of trauma, required, I found, constant, wearying propitiation – editing, remaking and rubbing out in communication.

Without that peat bog of entanglement, the mess that was her, I sense my brother and I were snipped off into the white air, groundless and quite unable to manipulate language in a way that felt spontaneous and meaningful to those who, we sensed, were really only pulled to us by the power of the event itself.

The reaction of some of my loftier friends from that time to my daughter, brought back the time of our own destruction viscerally. At the same time I felt immense guilt, shame about my bizarre, paranoid reaction to their interventions, which felt extreme. Surely the ideal in the white world of pure spirit, of terror, was to love those who loved my children? Was I robbing my daughter of her ideal potential by emotionally, albeit involuntarily, blocking these birds that swooped on her? Sethe strangling Beloved at the bridge. Enforcing the singularity of the black hole. The ugly mark of maternity, the barrier to the world of forms, that is humanity. Saying for her, what no one said for me?

Stop! She's mine!

One night I woke with sobs so loud and wild that my real, living daughter herself woke, came in and held my hand and told me very kindly and strongly no one was going to take her, that she had no strong feelings about any of my spirit friends, whom she hardly knew. Anyway, she had her own friends.

I watched the penguins with horror and the orangutans with horror and I watched the little parcels of treasures coming for my daughter, my work of art, my own free spirit, with the pretty, thick wrapping papers carefully chosen and the cold, careful avoidance of me (no doubt to do in part with my rage). And I began to understand, just before I went mad myself, something of what was occluded in the spirit world, why every word we want to speak dissolves there, and why it is a perfect dream, unrecordable in the philosophy of language.

MOTHER HEN

How many times, did your strong hands
open the coop, feel broodiness like pain?
'She's flat as an iron, and ruckling again!
Hootling! And vague! And staring into space!'
You scooped me up, put me out to stand
in the slimy yard, on corn swollen by rain,
among the staring eyes and crenellated faces.
You took the fragile floor, I was not allowed
to own the orbed ellipse between my legs...
still I returned and flattened out a place –
though it was empty – made my mind a cloud
soft willing curves to layer in smooth white eggs
to grow, to crunch to bloody life in no one's hand.

★

Outside, in the rain, shaking the corn, you stand.
This weak, ungifted and ungenerous poem,
reminds me of that time of all of our blurred
spirit borders. Also of the suffering of broodiness, the way it clots the earth into a generality,
focusing the mind on the egg's ellipse. Broodiness is a difficult urge to break in a chicken.
People place broody chicks in wire based cages to prevent them lying down. Sometimes it
seemed to me, at bad times, as if my friends
were locked in so many wire cages to control
and spot target their desire.

I am still working this out. I made a ring, a
strong boundary around my children drawing
in a sense on my sister's ghost, her absence; I
could not lose what I loved most again. But I
cannot dismiss the white space of explosion
– the world of pure spirit – where we all met
– where boundaries evaporated – so that years
later those hands could creep right down inside my box. Heidegger may not write about
the spirit because ultimately it does annihi-

late being. As a child, being taken by the spirit world was my biggest fear (along with my whole family dying). I used to imagine, as an infant, that spirits visited me and chilled my back and was terrified I would be lost forever. Even Disney gives Elsa an Anna, to hold her out on her icy dazzle with the arms of home, but I did not have an Anna anymore. I needed my children. Enough to move away from my own terror.

Transcendence. Spirit. White vanishing. The space of fear outside language. I do not dismiss it because, looking at what happened to everybody else in my family after that explosion, I think, among many other things, although it unravelled into film, it might have saved my life.

10. THE BULLY

All chickens, in my experience, all of them, have a sense of pecking order and a capacity to bully those below. In my repeated experience, the most bullying hens are, invariably, rescues themselves – those home-bred are less aggressive. In the pen, I observe all hierarchies are liable to change, most quickly; as long as a chicken survives, it is likely to have a chance at some point to become the boss.

Turn.

The crisis in the spirit world seems now so small a thing. Light as a feather, a keratin ladder from nowhere to nowhere. It came through one of my friends from that time of explosion, at university. In a sense for the purpose of my story, to show the work of mourning, it doesn't matter who. Except in my heart she seemed literally like a frozen shadow of my dead sister, also a doctor – with similar big puffy hair and size – so literally her shadow, semblable, from Oxford. It also came out of a threat of repetition, one of us appeared to be terminally ill and had told almost no one – she seemed abstracted, unengaged as if she did not understand the import of the news and I got angry. She told me, as if she had been calculating me for some time, she had 'never liked me' really and formally terminated our friendship. She added that it was fine for my daughter to keep texting and Instagramming her. I did not understand her. Or know why.

Splinter from another break.

'O my friends, there are no friends!' The terrible paradox of human love collapsed into a flexing paranoia, like a flutter of bird shapes around my daughter for whom I knew my bonds were necessary and clean. My reaction was extreme,

I had no emotional separation from it at all. I felt close for the first time to the self despairing agony of a bullied teenager. At night I felt a sickening falling, more in the Miltonic than the Alice Oswald sense, to be honest, and in the day I began to live with a lasting new profound perpetual unreality, of disassociation.

I found myself searching as I fell at night, or early in the morning, for the reasons why this friend had made her decision. I took myself desperately back to my first introduction to her at university, and to the chicken yard, just before my sister was blown up – someone with a sad story – she had been bullied at school, I could not imagine it, still have my school friends, so could pity it easily. As a result, I had been told, she had developed anorexia. Spirit eyed, shy mouthed, vulnerable, I treated her, sentimentally perhaps, idealistically certainly, with special care and conscious intimacy. I could certainly identify with her anorexia, the signalling of a too sudden sense of separation, through refusing other intake to the body. After the explosion that took away my sister, I lost a stone in three days and my periods stopped for years. Eating was hard and I felt very self conscious, there was a black line between me and other things, I can still re-conjure at will.

What I could not understand was how this figure, one of the etched Nagasaki shapes, the permanent shadows, as I thought, burned onto my heart from the explosion of my sister, could decide for reasons that are still fairly opaque to me – for how in all goodness does one decide such a thing – after decades, holidays, support through dysfunctional husbands, that she wanted to end the friendship? As you might, say, end a subscription. It wasn't completely sudden, there were warnings for months, but because something like this had never happened to me before, I do not come from a cancel culture, I did not absorb them. I did not, for a moment, understand that I myself might be leaving the spirit world, or that as I was angry, so she might be. Nor that her own link to the event of my sister's death was her own, instinctive, justifiable, need for political voice.

So at first, I felt her withdrawing as dying, as if something very sad and reverend was happening to her, something that all my instincts fought against. As if she cared about me. What I found hardest to understand was the way that she would not engage in discussion about what clearly was an absolute and one-sided change of heart towards me. A decision. So strange, after decades. I was flooded with the pathos of her withdrawal, drawn to it as similarly, and helplessly, I have felt during long hours wetting and stirring chicken powders and tonics, trying to drip feed the broody starver, or the throat sick. I wrote poem after poem about the grief of her pulling away. I felt, so important did I believe our relationship to be, that she was committing a kind of Jain Sallekhana in front of me – like the most passive herbivores, sheep, chickens, she had decided to fade away.

I remember returning and returning at that time to the analogy of the bird, because it felt to me as if there was something imprinted, something instinctive in her withdrawal, that I could not reach emotionally, however hard I tried. I remember thinking, very clearly, 'You have done this elsewhere, before'. What amazed me was that she was removing herself from me as an act of will, her will, completely askance mine. She told me to 'be better without me'. As if she only saw herself as some kind of guide over dead space. It was difficult to reconcile with any kind of living, reciprocal friendship.

I am not proud of how long it took me to realise that my extreme reaction, waking to my own falling early each morning, weeping wildly at strange times of the day, was the result of earlier trauma, the fear I was losing my sister again. Or how slow I was to realise that what this woman, this ghost in place of my sister, chose to do to me was not only strange but also quite unkind. She was not actually just fading away. The opposite. Lightning, trapped bird, dead creature. Spirit world and my whole family dying. All my fears. She told me very specifically she was leaving because she 'did not like me' and, to make the situation ridiculous, she had 'never liked me'. That, though I was trying with all my might, in her view and at her injunction, I must somehow 'be better'. There was nothing I could do. Nothing felt or *reciprocal* about her announcement. The reason I was writing poem after poem (many, many, more, mostly avian!) was because they were all I had to hold her, since I did not have the words to explain to her she had burned to her very shadow in me at that moment of traumatic vanishing. I had nowhere to go back to. I loved her, so I thought, as I loved my sister.

And I had, at this point in my life, to understand miserably that to bully as a human is to subtly intuit the other's worst fear, and when that is grasped, O flesh spider! O human hand!

To trigger it. The child's hunger for excitement, explosion – raising the unreachable father locked in the study – tying the firework to the tail of the cat – married to the social insights of the grown up mad. And so, very calmly, with cool unconcern, as an act of will in fact, this woman 'detonated' me. She told me, she who was there at the explosion that she wanted to end our friendship, she had never liked me, carefully, she was happy to keep knowing my children, and then disappeared. Little china egg in the flames. Neat, arrogant, clear, little porcelain wall against the atom bomb of Naga-saki. The consequence was not as she hoped I don't think (hers was not a hopeful act) but as she, thrillingly, sensed.

Grief, loss, abandonment, confusion, death, de-spair exploded in me for a very long time. I lived again what I had lived, or had not lived, lived and not lived, because of the white spirit world, when my sister blew up. As she withdrew her-self, intently, purposefully from me, and I kept trying to understand and undo whatever it was I was doing wrong, I finally realised, through this truthful poem actually, it was not, or not only, she who was dying, it was also my throat that was being broken. That very simply at the moment of death, this is the loss.

BULLYING

I was laid out flat on the dry earth of the yard.
Once she had stretched out my neck,
I did not want to move. My whole body was tame,
I felt the broom handle on my neck,
My neck began to clench, she hesitated,
Then she returned, inside, to check her technique,
I lay there still, uneasy, on the warm ground.
She came back, lifted her foot and almost daintily,
With a swift precision, put all her small body weight
Upon my neck. I did feel the crack. Like a sudden
          blinding
Pain, saw sudden white and black, my whole body

Trembling, in a spasm, beating up dust.

  'Just the nerves,' she said.

I felt it all. The green earth sliding away.

The green earth slid away. I fell. Years on, I do think this woman's behaviour was particularly cruel and feel nothing but a kind of wary curiosity, she was a shadow of a shadow, playing a role I do not believe either of us fully understood. But I also see how, like Fizzy the cockerel and my husband, like the hands of my daughter-lifting power friends, she forced me back to re-confront the effects of my sister's death and my first breaking from the earth. The fallacy of the spirit world. I was too far out on the ice, too exposed. I saw the adamantine pressure I had placed on those whom I imprinted, who I believed air burned and present in my mourning space, long after they actually had needed to fly off, or knock themselves out on the glass, or sing their lovely song to the sky. In that sense, my spectral figure's act of cruelty released me, or began my release from the high white trap, the world of guides, of being a chicken, of fear, where nothing ever happens. Of terror. Where I began.

For this act of course finally forced me to realise, that each spirit who guided me, held, as vanished terror, a shadow very silent, huge and difficult of their own. Usually the shadow of a difficult or cruel or, in the kindest guides, missing, mother. That the explosion which had displaced me into an Arctic Circle, was for them, in some sense, a more permanent state. The reason they walked like ghosts, geistlich, spirits of terror, through my blood bonds, was because they genuinely didn't, couldn't see, or possess, or feel them. Once I realised that, I began to hear the shadows, the unmarked traumas, the weariness, like my own, in their voices. Though I tried to continue, to follow, on the principle, I thought, of love, of imprinting, I couldn't. It was as if my legs had fallen off at the end of a dream and I was indeed falling awake.

11. ON VOICE

But this is not ten chapters but a dozen and the story does not end with the mud and the chickens and the falling awake that is the leaving of the world of pure terror.

VOICE

I didn't give him an inch – fit as he was –
Long legged Rouquin – because a
White bird flopped in Pieta
From his mouth. I made a banshee woop.
He dropped her and ran. She was the one
To speak. The one with holes in her neck
And bottom stripped out bare and pink.
She said, from the ground, you cannot know
What languages you speak, or what you have
To say, until you put yourself right back in this place –
With pity, rage, and claim to life at play.

Those white curls he pulled from her – her trace –
Lasted – long after she went in to lay.

This poem, which I like, came out of one of the strangest chicken incidents I have lived through. I was working in the kitchen when I suddenly heard a ruckus in the yard. Hens give a satisfied, melodious chortling, sequential and repetitive if they have laid an egg. A very different sound now, this chaotic, loud emergency!

I put my head out of the door and in the yard, with a white chicken flopping from its mouth, stood a fox. It froze when it saw me – bright orange, long-legged, skinny. We locked eyes.

Then something happened that none of us was expecting.

I began to make a noise.

Until that moment, I did not know I knew how to speak fox. At that moment I did. I began to make a noise that was high and wide and strange and yelping.

It was so strange a noise, that my daughter upstairs recorded it – thinking it was a child or other-world creature on the path by our house. And what I banshee yodelled, ululated to the fox was, be of no doubt, 'Drop the chicken, you fucker!'

And he did.

He dropped the chicken and ran off. The white chicken (who later was the one bullied by a cockerel) far from committing Sallakhana with shock or scattering her bleeding self along the hedgerows, though she did have a sore bare bottom and holes in her neck, walked back to the flock. A few days later she was laying again.

I was not sure why at the time this incident mattered so much. But I sensed it did. Voice, key to community living and democratic participation. The thing that my guides told me I lacked, and that went, my sense of speech evaporating inward. What I lost, when my sister was killed and my family disappeared as it seemed onto the white screen, and I into white fear and chicken keeping. What drew all those spirits to me, as if they were my friends or loves or angels, at the event. The seizure of the throat.

When I locked eyes with the fox, ruthless gift of nature, slivered from the wood, I saw, flopped, a white chicken and I knew, I knew what to say exactly, in his language, to make him put the chicken down.

And that, I think, is voice.

I am going to repeat it because it feels so important, for me anyway. To stare death in the eyes and tell it, in its own language of poisons, the pharmakon, to let life go. My daughter recorded the sound.

I understood this, a little later, in my own life. My brother from whom, like most grown brothers, I was life estranged, many years after my sister's death, seemed likely to die of the brain tumour that had begun to grow when our sister died, as it returned and many of the options for stopping it were exhausted. Simply, at that time, I felt him calling me. Not in an elegant or poetic way. Catastrophically and with my own heart. A consuming pain. Whole. Fuck the rest. I quietly let loose the weak string of my own life, the job I was half doing, even, emotionally, the relationship I had begun, and began the energy of the underwater fight where everything is slow and heavy, you've only got your own hands, and you know you'll die rather than give in. I put my energy into communication with him, releasing, erasing the walls of self that had kept me semi-upright, frozen since Lockerbie.

At the time, his wife said she knew he would be all right, it was 'something to do with Lockerbie'. I still feel now that he staged or sacrificed what he had in unspoken love to bring us back, spreading the wildly multiplying cells of his mind like a blanket to catch us all. Anyway, I went back. It was the situation – everything else felt relative, but this – below language and emotionally central – where I knew without the uncertainty that had dogged me since my sister's death. I made the decision however difficult things were, that I was going to stay with him. With all the force of my creation, with the resources I had, I told death to let him go. I didn't care. It could take me. It had to drop him.

But it seems to me now, as we met again in silence, may be with his own body, he was doing the same with me.

It was complicated. A messy sudden meeting, un-thought. A complicated dance. Reciprocal. My brother might have died but he did not die.

He is staying alive. I found, independently, my heart hurt and I had a voice that mattered, at least to him. I could use it and hear people. A gift from my brother. And I understood better what had happened that day in the yard, repeat,

VOICE

I didn't give him an inch – fit as he was –
Long legged Rouquin – because a
White bird flopped in Pieta
From his mouth. I made a banshee woop.
He dropped her and ran. She was the one
To speak. The one with holes in her neck
And bottom stripped out bare and pink.
She said, from the ground, you cannot know
What languages you speak, or what you have
To say, until you put yourself right back in this place –
With pity, rage, and claim to life at play.

Those white curls he pulled from her – her trace –
Lasted – long after she went in to lay.

12. THOUGHT

These dozen chapters, eggs, years, were hand written in a note book with a pencil. Eleven real poem apostles and a false one, based on a film about birds at the pole. Sensing that the only way I could get into them, close to them was by crawling and creeping out my flesh spider, my hands and groping in the dark to feel their cool ellipse.

When I was young, I remember a teacher I loved (with all the complexities of that), the only one at university who seemed to have some real sense of the indivisible explosion of terror in my head, listened to me and the experience of speaking to her, of finding words – making a poem at the time – felt like I was breaking words like eggs on her mind, the yolks running.

Since I was a teenager, I have incubated birds' eggs. I took some to Oxford once, in an incubator, wrapped in a blanket, I remember, before Lockerbie, my mother and I stopped for a coffee, lost the car keys, and had to wait hours, desperately, for the car to be opened again, with the eggs cooling in the back. We thought they may have died in the shell but I continued to water them and turn them dark/light and many hatched. At the beginning of lockdown we incubated hens' eggs, candling them to check on development, I made a loose simple sketch,

THOUGHT EGG

Our candling lights cathedrals in blood.

        Behind the porcelain rude screen a red, blue saint is trapped in her lead web…

we turn her, turn.

> The plaster wall flattens, flakes
> off a wind fluttering membrane…
> banner of wet boiling flesh…
>
> a black point crumbles to a broken
> line, a mouth that speaks her out
> in jerks…
>
> sticky, trembling –
> the walls smear with her – she staggers
> from the empty eyeball, the stained skull,
> small, air puffed,
> wobbly as a prayer…

The Thought Egg is hardly a poem. It notes the emergence of the last chicken I really bonded with, Bluey. But it also describes a holy space.

Of those eggs, the other two that hatched were cockerels, one of whom, like his father, was perhaps as beautiful as a bird can be, deep red rust flame and dove grey to cinder ash in a loose, floating fan of tail feathers.

I suppose one of the reasons I have ended my clutch on thought, rather than voice, is that I believe in it and its slow, unobservable evolution. For all its limitations, failures and paralysis. I still return to Hannah Arendt's perception after the Eichmann trials, that evil equates to weakness and conformity of mind, a willingness to obey commands rather than to think, watch, feel, think really think for yourself.

We live at a time that still echoes with Nike's (contemptible) *Just Do It!* and everyone – from my friends laughing at me for sitting by a little plastic reproduction of Izaak Walton studying 'to be quiet' given by a student I loved to teach, to George Ezra bemoaning this terrible time to be alive 'if you're prone to over-thinking' – seems wary, understandably, of the endless empty nothingness of the mind, the crippling self absorptions, hand right on top of the head. But I stand with Dante for 'il ben del intelletto', the shell and the albumen of the brain as the absorbent medium for terror. I think it's usually not the *thought*, but the *event* that cripples. The mind remains what is holy in us, in our short lives and for our brief species, it is not just our loveliest dream, it is our power to understand fear. *To under stand*. I believe it is the only means by which we can learn to do what is required of us, to connect the sky to the ground. However paltry. I observe with Hannah Arendt, despite her many caveats, that those who think in the long run, cannot only survive but do less to harm, to really *harm*, others.

In the end, the cockerels of ash and flame made too much noise and scuffed up the back of the hens too much. My friend Tasha (whose parents it turns out live in the house where Izaak Walton slept over when he went to catch and study fish, in some bafflement at humans and love of creatures) suggested we just release them in the local park. Her family had looked after a cockerel who just flew into their barn on his own accord, for years. Uneasily, I repeat, as we began, I advertised the two we owned, on-line preloved site. They both went, within a month of each other, to two little boys, Jan and Nima, whose families, from Poland and India, already had chickens and who thought it would be cool to have a rooster too. Nima arrived with his father at our house holding an enormous blown up paper photo of the specific cockerel he wanted, as if he was expecting an identity parade. Apparently the cockerels have settled in well. I do not know how much longer I will keep chickens myself.

Socrates as he was dying of poison he administered to himself, apparently said as his last words, 'Crito, I owe the sacrifice of a rooster to Asklepios; will you pay that debt and not neglect to do so?'

The meaning of these words remains very uncertain, but fixing my eyes on death – fear around me, surging in angel shapes in my head, my flesh spiders scuttling – I remember, not just those two cockerels of ash and flame, but a great body of living creatures who as a species have teamed endlessly to our cruelty and whim, and I am, like this chapter, in no doubt to whom, and for whom, I sacrifice the rooster.

APPENDICES

* *The rest of the draft poem turned up folded in a book of maps*

…are clenched within their claws; yet; they do seem,
how to say it, surprisingly palpitant, surprisingly, warm and close,
as they sit deep in the arm fold, their eyes round,
black and wet with presence; whether you have outstretched
to cut their (glorious) wings or turned them rumpwards
for a check of vents.

This dream then; we avoid complicated
Victorian hybrids with posh names and leg feathers
to catch fleas (they are a very recent phenomenon;
the last two hundred, in eight thousand years of domesticity)

We pay two pounds. Rescue a bulb fried bird.
Its grey skin looks afraid; grey comb. It rasps; its beak's
cut. And yet. It eats. It is not a feather plucker or a fellow pecker.
It considers, then rejects, euthanasia. Slowly, its white skin
quickens into a down, the complex colour of which is

147

not done justice by the word chestnut. Nor the size and gloss.
Its willingness to communicate in clucks every exit and entrance
would be reward enough. Only the eggs; fist fat, rollicking, luscious,
twin yolked and with a taste that makes (all our friends say)
Boxed, Free-Range, Organic, taste like water standing too long
      in a can.

So I dreamed. The fox came last night.
Split our coop and killed each bird on its perch. Just for fun.

EPILOGUE

My mother, who I love, has asked me to write an addition to this book explaining that 'putting emotions into print tends to give our constantly variable and changeable feelings the sort of permanence they do not always deserve.' We agree that the feelings we have for ourselves are impermanent. But so are we. And, once we open our mouths, potentially kitsch, ridiculous, terrified and infinitely consumable. Sometimes, I, personally, have found acknowledging our constantly variable feelings, helps. The value or otherwise of these twelve eggs is for the reader to decide.

ACKNOWLEDGEMENTS

For all the insularity and parochialism of my subject I owe a lot of amazing people from many places big thanks.

In particular – Marina Kolchanova, Lisa Barton, Alice Wallbank, Helen Barr, Bridget Macdonald and Tsering Gellek, for being such thoughtful and encouraging early readers. Sally McCleery for extraordinary editorial acumen and needle sharp critique. Ro and Leah, Alison Jones, John Elcock for wise advice. Tom McCleery and Isobel Mason for thoughtful, astute young eyes. Alice and Matthew for their friendship. Vyara Popova and Ekaterina for their faith and for understanding the importance of names. Dmitri for laughing at Fizzy. Grace and Sam for their essential love and support, my family for allowing it – and Ian for taking it.

And thank you to the team at the Black Spring Press Group, especially Matt the cover designer, Edwin the typesetter, and Amira, Cate and Todd, who helped with the editing and proofreading.